I Will
Not Bow

I Will Not Bow

NAN M. PAMER

I Will Not Bow

by Nan M. Pamer

©1997 Word Aflame Press
Hazelwood, MO 63042-2299

Printing History: 1997

Cover Design and Photography by Paul Povolni
Cover Photo of Holly Duncan, granddaughter of E. J. McClintock

All Scripture quotations in this book are from the King James Version of the Bible unless otherwise identified.

Printed in United States of America.

Printed by

Library of Congress Cataloging-in-Publication Data

Pamer, Nan M.
    I will not bow : / by Nan Pamer.
        p.   cm.
    ISBN 1-56722-203-X
    I. Christianity and culture—United States. 2. Christian life—
Pentecostal authors. 3. Mass media—United States—Influence.
4. Clothing and dress—Religious aspects—Christianity. 5. Holiness—
Christianity. I. Title.
BR115.C8P32   1997
243—dc21   97-9330
                                                                  CIP

Dedicated to
our children,
Alyson, Paul and Rose

Contents

Introduction

Don Feder, author of _Who's Afraid of the Religious Right_, had the opportunity to interview Charlton Heston, the noted actor. Mr. Feder, a Jewish man of great faith in God, could not resist asking Mr. Heston this question: "Did playing Moses in the film _The Ten Commandments_ change you in any way?"

Mr. Heston laughed and replied, "Well, one thing changed. I no longer received invitations to Hollywood parties. But let's face it, when someone is fooling around with another man's wife, he doesn't want to look across the room and see Moses!"

Whether Mr. Heston realized it or not, his comment was insightful and has far-reaching implications concerning the world of entertainment. Hollywood and its outgrowth has become an enormous kingdom, with tentacles reaching every corner of the modern world. It has slowly and methodically set forward an agenda of bringing everyone to conform to its viewpoint, and that agenda is filled with violence, lust, and pride.

To "look across the room" and see religious people who will not reflect their agenda, who refuse to bow to their immoral lifestyle and image, is troubling to the entertainment kingdom. When religious people reflect their faith in their outward appearance, it reminds the ungodly of a holy God who has set forth laws of morality and righteousness, and it makes them uneasy.

> To "look across the room" and see religious people who will not reflect their agenda, who refuse to bow to their immoral lifestyle and image, is troubling to the entertainment kingdom.

Along with the kingdom of entertainment, another kingdom has taken prominence in the twentieth century, the fashion industry. The fashion world froths with greed and immorality. It is a world where image is everything. It, too, despises "looking across the room" and seeing those who refuse to reflect what it promotes.

These two kingdoms of the world have radically changed the way people think and act in America. They are modern in appearance but ancient in their motives, which are to reflect wickedness in what they produce and to bring to their knees all those who refuse to bow down but who stand for righteousness. At the core of their philosophy is the desire to destroy what is righteous and God-conscious, including matters of outward appearance.

In the earlier decades of this century, those who lived dedicated lives and reflected God in their outward appearance were held in high esteem even by corrupt and evil people, but that is no longer true today. Whether we recognize it or not, there is a growing spirit of disdain and contempt toward godly people. No doubt, the pressure to conform to the world's image will grow stronger and stronger as evil people wax worse and worse. The world will not announce to the church, "Because you are righteous, we will attempt to change you," but rather this message will come in subtle forms of intimidation.

Christian people who desire to reflect God and His Word in their outward appearance must be aware of what is taking place. To continue to honor God in this manner will require tremendous grit and fortitude. We will be told of our irrelevance and our lack of education. We will be accused of being legalists, cultists, and Pharisees; told that we look ugly; and told that we are out of step. These are weapons of intimidation by a world that wants all that is good to bow down. The method is different, perhaps, but the desire is the same: to destroy the influence of godly people.

The purpose of this work is first to encourage the precious saints of God who have refused to bow to the pressures of the world. They are my heroes and I give honor to them. Secondly, I hope in some small way to expose the enemy's strategy so that no one will fall prey to it. We are commanded to be aware of his devices, and I pray that they are revealed in this effort.

Chapter 1

Spiritual Wickedness in High Places

The church of Jesus Christ must be aware of what is taking place in the realm of the spirit. We are not fighting flesh and blood, but principalities and powers, rulers of darkness, and spiritual wickedness in high places, and the fashion and entertainment industries are instruments of these principalities. To wipe out the righteous influence of godly people is their goal.

The constant stream of lustful images in the fashion and entertainment worlds, their relentless persuasion to find pleasure in material things, and the entertainment world's emphasis on murders and killings are all indications that they are motivated by the ruler of darkness, Satan. Some may scoff at naming the devil as the basic source of these institutions, but if we look at what is being produced, it is easy to see there is a great wickedness at their roots.

Let us notice what the temptation of Jesus reveals concerning this subject:

"Again, the devil taketh him up into an exceeding high mountain, and sheweth him all the kingdoms of the world, and the glory of them; and saith unto him, All these things will I give thee, if thou wilt fall down and worship me. Then saith Jesus unto him, Get thee hence, Satan: for it is written, Thou shalt worship the Lord thy God, and him only shalt thou serve" (Matthew 4:8-10).

This was a decisive moment in history. The embodiment of all that was good and righteous came face to face with all that was bad and evil in the world. Jesus Christ, the second Adam, met the great tempter, who had won the first round in the Garden of Eden. The devil apparently thought he could deceive Jesus Christ as quickly as he had Adam and Eve.

This passage of Scripture reveals three very important points:

1. The devil directs the kingdoms of this world and uses their glory to tempt us.

This third temptation was the final and greatest thing that Satan could offer Jesus Christ. It was his *coup de gras*, his last and most grandiose offer. "If you will bow down to me, I'll give you my kingdoms!" The devil gleefully laid down his most precious gift, thinking no one alive could possibly refuse such an offer. By this remark, the devil betrayed his influence over the kingdoms of this world, which include the entertainment and fashion industries. Satan uses these kingdoms in an attempt to intimidate the church.

2. The devil's deepest desire is to bring what is good and holy down to its knees before him.

As Jesus Christ was poised to begin His public ministry, immediately the devil came, wanting Him to fall down and worship him. Because He was the embodiment of goodness, Jesus Christ was Satan's most sought-after foe. Since the beginning, it has been the devil's mission to bring down to its knees all that is good. From Adam and Eve to the apostle Paul, much of the Bible's historical record deals with the enemies of God working to bring the people of God under their subjection. Whenever a man or woman rose from the circumstances to stand for righteousness, immediately a pushing began, a pressure to give in.

> It was the only response that our righteous Savior could give. To have given in the slightest amount would have destroyed His mission to restore humanity's relationship with a holy God. Jesus is our perfect example and we must follow Him.

Nothing infuriated Goliath quite like the boy David standing up to him. The kingdoms of this world have always despised those who refused to bend and still today are enraged by those who dare to be different and refuse to bow down to the dictates of the world.

3. Jesus Christ would not bow to the enemy.

When Jesus Christ said no to the devil's final and greatest offer, undoubtedly the enemy left in a fit of rage and disbelief. Though Satan had brought thousands to their knees, he could not bend the Lord's one degree. It was the only response that our righteous Savior could give. To have given in the slightest amount would have destroyed His mission to restore humanity's relationship with a holy God. Jesus is our perfect example and we must follow Him.

For those in the church of Jesus Christ who have not conformed to the kingdoms of this world, the enemy is still furious. He has launched an all-out assault to force the church to bow down. Darkness has declared war on the light!

The Kingdoms of This World

Over the last twenty-five years, the worlds of fashion and entertainment have exposed their true nature. These institutions are incredibly immoral and decadent. It is more than coincidence that they reflect the devil's nature: arrogant, lustful, full of pride, and totally refusing to regard God in any manner. These kingdoms belong to him.

The apostle Paul gave an interesting description in II Timothy 3 of people in the last days:

1. Lovers of their own selves
2. Lovers of pleasures more than lovers of God
3. Boasters, proud, blasphemers, false accusers, heady, high minded, and so on

The kingdoms of fashion and entertainment embody these descriptions! Michael Medved's book *Hollywood vs. America* documents how Hollywood attacks religion, derides patriotism, glorifies brutality, and undermines the family with its vicious attack on morality. Does that not sound like the archenemy of Christ?

> The pressure to conform to the world's image is greater than ever, due in part to the proliferation of television throughout our culture.

The pressure to conform to the world's image is greater than ever, due in part to the proliferation of television throughout our culture. As part of the entertainment kingdom, television is relentless in shoving its philosophy down America's throats. An image is set forth through programming and advertising that demands conformity. If men and women do not have the look of this image, they are branded irrelevant and inconsequential.

That Calvin Klein, a leading fashion designer, would use children in seductive poses in order to sell his fashions, speaks volumes as to the basic nature of the fashion industry. Some of the most immoral designers are the ones who place their name all over their products. Such arrogance and pride should alert us to who is promoting these things: Lucifer, prince of pride. We can read the newspaper on any given day and find numerous examples of the incredibly wicked lives many of these people live, breaking all ten commandments daily! These institutions are at odds with Jesus Christ and His church, and they will do anything to wipe out Christ's influence in the world today.

Chapter 2

"Bow Down!"

Those who refuse to be intimidated by the world and choose to stand for godliness will be challenged by the kingdoms of this world.

Our North American culture is spiritually bankrupt. The sins of all generations seem to have accumulated in the last decade of the twentieth century. In this setting especially, all Christians should be dramatically different from the world, following Christ's example and refusing to be intimidated by the devil. Yet many times, instead of clashing with the world, churches have compromised and bowed to the pres-

> Those who refuse to be intimidated by the world and choose to stand for godliness will be challenged by the kingdoms of this world.

sure of the world.

The Christian church must realize that those who refuse the world's standards often stand alone. We must get used to it. Noah stood alone in the world before the flood, Elijah on Mt. Carmel, John the Baptist in the face of religious leaders, Stephen in a hostile first century, and a host of others. They were ridiculed by the culture and misunderstood by their peers, but that did not change them.

If one's faith isn't challenged by this wicked, evil, perverse culture, something is wrong. Christ's church should always be at odds with the culture. Satan is the prince of this world, his will is carried out in the institutions of this world, and the church must never allow itself to be influenced by them.

There are no lions in coliseums facing those who refuse to conform to the ideal set forth by these establishments, but there is a very real force coming against those who reflect God in their appearance. These kingdoms are savage in their desire to make everyone bow down and worship them. Paul also referred to the world in the last days as being "despisers of those that are good" (II Timothy 3:3). We should not think it strange that our desire to honor God in an outward appearance is not appreciated. We should expect such a reaction from the world.

The Spirit of Mordecai

Mordecai, from the Book of Esther, lived in a situation similar to ours today. The citizens of Shushan did not regard God in any area of their lives. Mordecai was ignored and deemed irrelevant by the culture. Yet he quietly and steadfastly honored God by doing what was right, whether it was raising his orphaned niece (2:7) or reporting a conspiracy against the king (2:22). While Mordecai was a good and honorable man, his refusal to bow infuriated Haman, a wicked man whose very fiber reeked of pride and arrogance. "And when Haman saw that Mordecai bowed not, nor did him reverence, then was Haman full of wrath" (Esther 3:5).

Haman embodied the spirit of the world. He hated Mordecai for refusing to bow to him. It would have been so much simpler if this godly man would have given in on this matter, but there were things in his life that he could not compromise. Mordecai was not spiritually arrogant, though some might have interpreted his actions that way. He continued what he had always done, honoring God's law in every way he could regardless of the consequences. That kind of faith will always infuriate the prince and power of this age.

Haman was an Agagite, probably of the descendants of Agag, a common name of the princes of Amalek (Numbers 24:7). This point is very interesting because of the Amalekites it was written, "The LORD will have war with Amalek from generation to generation" (Exodus 17:16). "Remember what Amalek did unto thee by the way, when ye were come forth out of Egypt" (Deuteronomy 25:17).

Amalek came against Moses and Israel in an unprovoked attack during a difficult period of their history, and God did not want His people to forget the deadly assault.

Mordecai immediately discerned that the spirit of Amalek was still very much alive in Haman, and he would not bow. The moment Mordecai took his stand, Haman's true nature immediately showed. He devised a plan to wipe out the Jewish nation. The spirit of Amalek was working.

The war that Haman declared on the Jews was provoked by one insignificant Jew who would not bow down. Thousands bowed on the streets of Shushan, but that one man's refusal infuriated Haman.

The spirit of Amalek, the spirit of Haman, and the spirit of Satan are the same. We must not forget the destructive nature of these spirits. They long to destroy and bring to its knees everything good.

> The enemy is infuriated every time Apostolic teenagers refuse to be like everyone else.

This force is very much at work in our world today. The enemy is infuriated every time Apostolic teenagers refuse to be like everyone else, and he declares an all-out war to bring them to their knees. He has launched an assault to force the church to bow down. Darkness has declared war on the light!

This attack should not invoke any fear in a Christian's heart, but rather it should reveal what is transpiring in the spirit world. We must be aware of the devil's devices; otherwise we will not understand the tug-of-war taking place in our minds. Thoughts of compromising, giving in, or relenting must be labeled correctly; they are the fiery darts of the devil seeking to destroy our faith in

God and His Word and bring us to our knees. While the spirit of Amalek, the spirit of Haman, and the spirit of Satan has worked throughout history to wipe out godly influence from the world, it has failed. It has never been able to touch a child of God who is standing! We need not be afraid of its threats and intimidations, for God will take care of us.

Darkness has declared war on the light!

Matthew Henry in his commentary on the Book of Esther said of Mordecai, "He was adhering to his principles with a bold and daring resolution." "Bold and daring resolution" is an oddity in our culture. Tolerance, acceptance, and "go with the flow" have become the ruling schools of thought. That type of mindset does not produce people like Mordecai. "Bold" is one of the words often mentioned in describing the early Christians, and it behooves the Christians of today to develop this characteristic in their lives. The enemy's methods may have changed, but his motive remains unchanged, namely, to bring down what is holy. It will take a bold and daring resolve to defeat him.

Chapter 3

The Blessed Refusal

I belong to a religious group, Apostolic Pentecostals, that has refused to conform. We are not the largest group in number, but because we will not bow, we are being pressured relentlessly. That opposition puzzled me for some time until I studied the temptation of Jesus and understood the nature of the ruler of darkness. He is a devourer. He hates all that is good and holy, and his very nature requires that he destroy it. He will do anything to wipe out our influence with whatever methods he can.

At the beginning of the twentieth century when the Holy Ghost was poured out, those who received the new birth experience immediately forsook the influences of the world's systems and sought diligently to reflect God and His Word in every aspect of their lives. However, as the years have gone by, the pressure to conform gripped the twentieth-century Christian church. By the 1960s, most Holiness and Pentecostal groups, many whose roots were in the Topeka and Azusa Street revivals, had forsaken all outward manifestations of an inward holiness. To see them on the street, one could not tell the difference between saint and sinner.

The Apostolic Pentecostal movement has remained firm and refused to allow the world to dictate their lifestyle. Because we have entered into the last days of this century, I believe Apostolic Pentecostals have been marked for annihilation by the kingdoms of this world. Perhaps some would say that I am being overly dramatic, but the relentless assault to give in is more than a flesh-and-blood battle. It is in the realm of principalities and powers. We are the greatest bastion still standing that makes an effort to reflect God and His Word against the kingdoms of this world. The devil wants us out of the way.

> When a Christian weakens on an issue, all hell notices and comes running, relentlessly hounding until all resemblance of godliness is gone.

Vulnerability to the Enemy

We as Apostolic people adhering to a biblical code of living must firmly stand against this onslaught. It is the only thing we can do, because if we weaken on a single issue, the pressure will increase tenfold. With giving in to pressure, comes a weakness and vulnerability to the enemy. Do we think that laying down one conviction will be the end of compromise? Will the pressure stop if we give ground? That is very unlikely. Bowing to the force of conformity throws up a white flag that is recognized throughout the spirit realm. A stalking lion watches for weakening signs of his fleeing prey. It thrills the lion and invigorates him. So it is with the stalkers of Satan's kingdom. When a Christian weakens on an issue, all hell notices and comes running, relentlessly hounding until all resemblance of godliness is gone.

II Kings 12 is an interesting chapter in the history of Israel concerning King Jehoash on the subject of giving in. Hazael, king of Syria and the enemy of God's people, set his face against Jerusalem to destroy it. Instead of fighting and standing against this enemy, King Jehoash took every hallowed, consecrated, dedicated treasure in the house of the Lord and the king's house and handed it over to the king of Syria without a fight! King Jehoash succumbed to the pressure of the world and lost every sacred thing he possessed, leaving himself and his kingdom impoverished. The sad ending to this account is that one year later, the host of Syria returned, destroying the prince and plundering the city (II Chronicles 24:23-24).

The American patriot Thomas Paine, when faced with the armies of destruction coming against our young nation, wrote, "'Tis the business of little minds to shrink; but he whose heart is firm, and whose conscience approves his conduct, will pursue his principles unto death." As a member of our Apostolic Pentecostal movement who feels the pressure to conform, I must declare,

"My heart is firm and my conscience approves my conduct." Thus I will not bow down to the institutions of this world that are trying to wipe out all reminders of a holy God who has called out a holy people. The church is feeling the pressure to change, to bow to the pressure of the institutions of this world. It takes a brave heart in any age to stand against such a crowd, but God requires that if we are to be His, we must not bow.

> " 'Tis the business of little minds to shrink; but he whose heart is firm, and whose conscience approves his conduct, will pursue principles unto death."
>
> T. Paine

Thousands Bowed

The Book of Daniel contains one of the most thrilling and awe-inspiring accounts in antiquity concerning the refusal to conform.

Shadrach, Meshach, and Abednego were labeled odd from the beginning. They arrived in Babylon as prisoners of war from the land of Israel. There were no parents directing them or strong leaders instructing them. While they could have blended in with the culture and forgotten all their teachings from the past, they instead refused to eat the king's food, a minor but important discipline of Israel. They didn't rail at their captors or whine about their restrictions; they simply would not break the law of God.

Many Babylonians dismissed them as unenlightened

foreigners who were out of touch with modern society. They noticed their vitality and health, benefits of their decision, but still counted the young men as ridiculously overcommitted. So it was no surprise to their peers when the three young Hebrews were marched out to the plain of Dura and commanded to bow before the gigantic image of Nebuchadnezzar, the embodiment of the world's systems of that day, that their knees didn't bend a degree.

Those youths deserved esteem and honor for standing in the face of their world's system and refusing to bow. It must have been embarrassing, intimidating, and very lonely to do so, but so noble! No, the world of Babylon did not understand them. All their friends in the world were on their knees, but these three heard the echo of an almost-forgotten archaic law that their parents had taught them: "Thou shalt have none other gods before me . . . Thou shalt not bow down thyself unto them" (Deuteronomy 5:7, 9). They simply could not bow.

The 3HC Mentality

The three young men had a marvelous ingredient in their lives: an intense love and respect for God and His Word. I call it the *3HC mentality*, the Three Hebrew Children mentality. While no one understood them, while it was only one point of the law, and while everyone they knew had his face down in the dirt of cowardice, mocking their resistance, these young men would not bow. "Thou shalt not have any other gods before me," was one of the ten basic tenets of their belief system, and they would not compromise.

Their bravery thrills me. It is the mentality I want my children to have! I do not want Alyson, Paul or Rose ever to bow down to the pressure of the world. A mentality that says, "It is written; thus I will live by it!" gets the attention of another world. My children may stand alone at the mall or on the campus when they stand for biblical principles, but there is an unseen host that stands by their side.

The three Hebrew children's refusal to become a part of the culture baffled the Babylonians. It was difficult for the world to understand why anyone would refuse to do something that everyone else was doing! A refusal to the world's kingdoms based on a love for God was totally perplexing then and throughout history. Rome could not understand why the first-century Christians could not serve Christ and also bow to Caesar. Today society does not comprehend the mindset of Apostolic Pentecostals who, because of our love for the Word of God and our desire to honor it, will not bow to the demands of this culture.

It is written; thus I will live by it!

The fashion and entertainment kingdoms have determined that there will be no distinctions between male and female, including their clothing and their hair. Our biblical beliefs that women should have long hair, that men should have short hair, and that there should be differences in their dress are totally unacceptable to the kingdoms of this world. We can do one of two things: we can give in and forsake our beliefs, or we can stand. But we can be assured, when unbelief meets convictions, there will be a struggle and a great contempt from the culture for our beliefs.

A Wicked Image

God was very specific about the Israelites reflecting Him in their outward appearance. The priests had very stringent rules for how they were to dress so that they might be a continuous reminder to the people of a holy God. Today, the church is God's royal priesthood, and we are still required to reflect God so that the world might see Him through us. However, we cannot forget that Satan has his own image that he wants reflected in the world today. It is lustful, arrogant, and vile.

> We can give in and forsake our beliefs, or we can stand.

When the Israelites reached Canaan, the Promised Land, they were instructed to break down and burn the images of the pagan cultures that surrounded them (Deuteronomy 7:5). This command reveals to us:

1. The pagan world had images that could adversely influence people.

2. God did not want His people to have anything to do with these images of the world.

Anat, Asherah, and Ashtaroth were three goddesses of the Canaanite pantheon. At various archeological sites in Palestine, images of these three have been found. These images of the female goddesses are usually naked or seminaked women with exaggerated physical features, and frequently their hands accentuate these areas.

The region of Canaan was filled with fertility cults that conducted sordid and perverse practices that were wicked beyond description, and they had images of their perverse gods, large and small, throughout their culture. Huge images looked down on the people in the temples, and small ones were kept in their homes. These images were important to the continuance of their pagan religion.

God forbade Israel to have anything to do with these images. They reflected sensuality, perversion, and a host of other wicked practices that God wanted to keep from Israel.

Of course, we are not living under the Mosaic law, so the church does not break up or burn images today. However, there is a principle in the Old Testament that carries over into the New Testament. The world today sets up an image on televisions, magazines, and billboards of how men and women should look that reflects its values and subtly calls for everyone to conform. But God's people are not to embrace this image:

"Love not the world, neither the things that are in the world. If any man love the world, the love of the Father is not in him. For all that is in the world, the lust of the flesh, the lust of the eyes, and the pride of life, is not of the Father, but is of the world" (I John 2:15-16).

We are not to love the things of the world, and that includes the images that the entertainment and fashion industries put before us. Keeping ourselves from that love enables us to manifest the love of the Father.

Contempt of the World

It was my family's dream vacation: two days on an island off the coast of Florida in a beachfront condominium. We were there with old friends and having the time of our lives. It was mid-August, much too hot for most people, but we didn't mind. The ocean was wonderful, whatever the temperature.

As we stood on the white, sandy beach listening to the marvelous roar of numberless waves hitting the shore, a man walked by, stopped, looked at our little group, and said to my husband, "Lose your luggage?"

Rod replied though confused, "No," momentarily not understanding his implication. The man looked puzzled and walked on, occasionally glancing back at our party, dressed modestly.

We then realized it was our unbeachlike clothes. Our clothes were light, but we were not in ordinary immodest beachwear. We all laughed but refused to be intimidated.

Out on the horizon a jet ski roared into view. My son, Paul, immediately responded with excitement, "Ahhh, Dad, let's try that."

Typically for my husband, the answer came, "Hey, we are on vacation! Let's do it!" and away went the guys of our group.

Upon arriving at the ski rental facility, a young beachcomber employee looked at Paul in his T-shirt and light but long pants and said in a condescending manner,

"What is it with you guys? Ya cold or what?"

Paul looked him in the eye and said, "No, this is what we want to wear," quickly realizing that the general consensus toward modesty was disdain.

"Well," replied the young man, "you look like fools!"

Thus we have in a nutshell what the general public thinks of my family's beliefs concerning modesty of dress and our refusal to conform to the world's standards. In fact, it sums up the world's opinion for much of our Pentecostal lifestyle.

Now, the question we must ask ourselves is this, "Do we change our beliefs? Do we cast off what we truly believe is God's will for Christian people, namely, that they dress modestly? Or do we brace ourselves and stand?"

Our family has chosen to brace ourselves and stand.

Unfortunately, many Christians have not realized what was happening when they felt the intense pressure to conform, and it has taken its toll on the Christian community. Many Christians have decided it is much easier on themselves and their children to rid themselves of practices that cause them to stand out in a crowd. They do not want to be ridiculed or made to feel uncomfortable by how they look. Looking different from the crowd puts one in a precarious position at times, but it is to be expected when the culture at large rejects biblical teaching.

When people begin to reflect the image of the world, they begin to take on the sins of that world. As a person begins to blend into the mosaic of the world, he or she becomes more comfortable with the world, gradually picking up the world's mannerisms and habits, and eventually becoming identical to them in every respect.

To Reprove Sin

For those who are filled with the Holy Ghost, to reprove sin is our mandate. Jesus told His disciples that He had to go away in order for the Comforter to come and that the Comforter would reprove a world of sin:

"Nevertheless I tell you the truth; It is expedient for you that I go away: for if I go not away, the Comforter will not come unto you; but if I depart, I will send him unto you. And when he is come, he will reprove the world of sin, and of righteousness, and of judgment" (John 16:7-8).

If the Holy Spirit dwells within a person, he will work in his life to reprove sin. It is the nature of the Spirit of God. We as Spirit-filled people are to bring conviction to a sinful world. As Matthew Henry wrote, we are to "make them to know their abominations."

When holy men and women walk into a room of godless people, the latter should feel some type of reproof in their souls for evil deeds. Too often, Christians seek simply to make sinners feel comfortable because they love them and want to reach out to them. Many believe that reaching out to comfort the sinner is the primary work of the Spirit, and certainly it is part of the Spirit's work. But that is not the only work of the Spirit. The Holy Ghost is a Comforter, but He is also a reprover. Far too many in Christendom have forgotten the *dual* duty of the Holy Spirit that Jesus taught: to comfort and reprove.

Chapter 4

Long Hair for Women

As a girl, I learned verses of Scripture that instructed me to regard God in everything I did. "In all thy ways acknowledge him, and he shall direct thy paths" (Proverbs 3:6). Longing to obey the commandments of the Bible, I made some commitments based on teaching from the New Testament.

One of the commitments I have made to God concerns my hair. I Corinthians 11 proclaims that long hair is a woman's glory, and I am committed to honoring God in that manner. The Scripture also says a woman ought "to have power on her head because of the angels," (I Corinthians 11:10). Apparently a woman's long hair gives her access to the protection and direction of angels. I have never been accosted in any manner, I have felt divine direction throughout my life, and I believe it is because of my relationship with God symbolized by my long hair. I have found enormous blessing in adhering to this passage of Scripture.

The Bible frequently mentions the work of angels in protecting and directing of God's people:

- *"And the angel of God, which went before the camp of Israel, removed and went behind them; and the pillar of the cloud went from before their face, and stood behind them"* (Exodus 14:19).

- *"For he shall give his angels charge over thee, to keep thee in all thy ways"* (Psalm 91:11).

- *"Blessed be the God of Shadrach, Meshach, and Abednego, who hath sent his angel, and delivered his servants that trusted in him"* (Daniel 3:28).

- *"My God hath sent his angel, and hath shut the lions' mouths, that they have not hurt me"* (Daniel 6:22).

- *"And, behold, the angel of the Lord came upon him, and a light shined in the prison: and he smote Peter on the side, and raised him up, saying, Arise up quickly. And his chains fell off from his hands"* (Acts 12:7).

- *"Are they not all ministering spirits, sent forth to minister for them who shall be heirs of salvation?"* (Hebrews 1:14).

The interest in angels that exists in the secular world is amazing. Many products display the image of angels, and yet our culture ignores the passage of Scripture that clearly states how people can truly have the attention and involvement of angels in their lives.

I Corinthians 11 teaches about the relationship between a husband and a wife, but the mention of the hair issue several times in this passage is enough to convince me of its importance. There is no question that women of the New Testament church had long, uncut hair. Yes, our culture has completely disregarded this teaching, but how can the modern church allow the world to steal from us a marvelous blessing from God?

The position that this teaching is cultural and should be ignored today is difficult to understand or accept. How can we take anything out of the New Testament and proclaim it cultural? The Epistles are God's letters to the church until He comes back.

I am thankful to belong to a group of Christians who did not draw that conclusion. They refused to accept the church world's decision on what is cultural! They were scoffed at, but thousands of Apostolic Pentecostal men and women have honored God with their hair, and they have reaped enormous blessing from it. When someone honors the Word of God in his or her life, there will be the favor of God.

The founders of the Apostolic Pentecostal movement also refused to accept the conclusions of theologians who said the gift of the Holy Ghost with the evidence of speaking in tongues was a cultural issue that belonged only to the early church. They simply chose to believe the Bible, and the Holy Ghost fell in Topeka, Kansas, and Azusa Street, forever changing religion's opinion of whether tongues are for today.

It must be noted that liberal theologians of Christendom no longer argue over such "irrelevant" points of Scripture as women's hair, but now have moved on to decide if Jesus was really born of a virgin, if the Bible is inerrant, and if ministers should be required to live moral, monogamous lives. When they decided that certain parts of the Bible were not important, they called into question the importance of many other passages.

Every verse is important, and none should be viewed as irrelevant. Perhaps if people had never viewed I Corinthians 11 as simply a forgotten custom, they would not dismiss other issues in the Bible.

Centuries of Women with Long Hair

For centuries women did not cut their hair. To a great extent American and European societies were biblically based, and Paul's writings in I Corinthians 11 were a way of life for women wanting to please God.

I enjoy reading about women who lived when there was still a widespread regard for God and His Word. Mrs. John D. Rockefeller, whose husband was an outstanding figure during the early twentieth century, from all appearances was a godly woman. Grace Goulder wrote:

> Everyone in describing Mrs. Rockefeller has spoken of her piety as wife and mother. The New Testament was the stanchion to which she anchored her daily life. Like her husband, she accepted the Bible literally as the inspired Word of God. Each day began with devotions at which the father presided. Each person, parents and chil-

dren alike, read a verse from the Bible. . . .
Worship ended, breakfast was served.
(*John D. Rockefeller*, Grace Goulder, 1971)

In every photograph, throughout her lifetime, she had her hair neatly fixed up on her head and uncut. She reflected what the majority of women believed in that time period: if the Bible addressed the matter of hair, then they could not ignore it.

Only in modern times has this view changed. The era that has seen unparalleled moral decay has also brought us the widespread practice of women having short hair. The era that threw out biblical teaching and brought in fornication, abortion, homosexuality, along with widespread venereal diseases, unparalleled teen pregnancies, and increased crime, has also brought us a new understanding for women concerning their hair. It also must be noted that many of these changes have been led by the movie industry.

> The era that has seen unparalleled moral decay has also brought us the widespread practice of women having short hair.

I choose to identify with women of past ages who regarded biblical teaching. Modern women have been wrong on a number of issues. For example:

- "Divorce is the answer for an unhappy marriage."
- "Leave small children to sitters while mothers pursue their careers."

• "Abortion is the answer for inconvenient pregnancies."

Women with little regard for God made these decisions, thousands followed, and the results have been devastating. Should these same women interpret I Corinthians 11 for the church?

Many American women have decided on short hair for convenience. Long hair is at times inconvenient, but when it comes to God's Word, there is a higher law than convenience. The things of God never fall into the easy and convenient category. If we are to be a living sacrifice, there are some things we do each day that are a sacrifice. This perhaps is a difficult concept for people who do not know Christ and His call to deny ourselves and take up our crosses, but for Christians it should be easily understood. While I understand the world's contempt for my long hair, I am puzzled when Christian people challenge my commitment to God concerning my hair.

> I want to be Jesus Christ's ideal woman, not the world's.

I sometimes imagine myself at the foot of the cross. It is a very sobering place. The things of the world are strangely dim. Fad and fashion have little influence there. In fact, the world's pressure to conform melts away. I want to be in His likeness, never the world's. I want to be Jesus Christ's ideal woman, not the world's.

When I allow my outward appearance to reflect a portion of God's Word, I am, in a small sense, letting the

Word become flesh. Dressing modestly, allowing my hair to grow long—issues addressed in the Bible—are very serious matters because the church is called to be a living epistle (II Corinthians 3:2). The Word of God is to be alive in us. Some Christians think this principle applies only to inward attitudes and issues such as gentleness, meekness, and temperance, but according to Scripture it also involves the outward issues of how we look. We will reflect the world or God's Word in our outward appearance. Which will it be?

Obedience is a peculiar word in this culture. So many people do not comprehend it, but it is still the summation of Christianity. Jesus was radically obedient. He was obedient unto death, agonizing in prayer in Gethsemane. He did not do His own will but the will of the Father. He was obedient to the law down to the last jot and tittle. Jesus Christ was obedient in every thought and motive, as well as deed. And we are required to be no less if we are His followers. We must be obedient to Christ and His Word.

"There is no escape from the responsibility of obedience." (See H. Richard Niebuhr, *Christ and Culture*, 1951.) My long hair is one way I honor God and His Word in my life. And while the world does not understand it, I am trying to follow a Christ-ordained obedience.

I have adhered to this discipline of having long hair and have known only protection and uninvolvement from the immorality that is deluging our nation. I have benefited by my obedience to God's Word concerning my hair. I have shared my beliefs with others, and they also have reaped enormous rewards from honoring Him. How could I disregard this blessing simply because the world does not agree? Only a foolish person would reject a way of life that has brought such enormous blessings to those who adhere to it.

The world's systems cannot stand someone bucking the tide. When the church rejects the image of the world, we must be ready for the intimidation and pushing that will come. As soon as the church feels the pressure to give in, we should position ourselves to stand firm.

For My Children

Jochebed, Moses' mother, when her child was in mortal danger, used a method that God had given Noah thousands of years before. She covered little Moses' boat with pitch, something that was waterproof and had been proven safe in times past. Noah's pitched boat had survived the greatest deluge of all time, and Jochebed trusted his proven method. Likewise the biblical standards I have given my children have been proven by generations of Apostolic people.

> It is not a good time for the church to try on the world's armor.

My late grandmothers, Nellie Beall and Eary Dyson, were Apostolic women who adhered to the biblical principles of modesty, and they had long, uncut hair. My mother, Marcella Dyson, and many of my aunts and cousins continued that tradition. They were never on the cover of a fashion magazine, but they were godly women whose lives were blessed in every aspect. One could easily see the blessings of God on their lives. I have seen living examples of what pleases God. How could I possibly reject such examples and begin to follow the world's leading on such issues as how I dress and wear my hair?

David could not wear Saul's armor because he had not proven it. David stood alone and God helped him, even with his seemingly out-of-date methods. I cannot take on a new lifestyle, a new way of dressing, a new way of wearing my hair.

The twentieth century is in chaos. Every aspect of American society shows signs of moral decay. It is not a good time for the church to try on the world's armor.

Chapter 5

Morality Dictates Theology

"**M**orality dictates theology" has often come to my mind when I ponder why the American church has laid down so many of its beliefs concerning outward appearance. This phrase says that the condition of one's heart determines how a person will interpret the Bible on such issues as separation from the world. However, I now realize that there is another slant to this understanding: children's morality dictates theology. In other words, many people revamp their theology because their children's morality has slipped. When people see their children questioning the standards of separation and sliding into the ways of the world, parents sometimes change their biblical understanding to justify their children's decisions.

This is a grave mistake. Children inherently question why we do things and often struggle with accepting patterns of living, but Moses addressed this issue centuries ago in Deuteronomy 6, saying in essence: When your children ask, "Why do we do the things we do? Why all the statues and laws?" tell them, "Because we were once in bondage and we never want to return to that. The only thing that will keep us from being enslaved again is to follow the law of God." (See Deuteronomy 6:20-21.)

Perhaps some Christians have decided to lay down the teachings that we as Apostolic Pentecostals adhere to because they have forgotten the bondage. They do not realize that if their children do not adhere to standards of separation, they will find themselves chained to a thousand devices of bondage, from alcoholism to pornography. God wanted the Israelites to be separate from the world because to take on all their ways was to ensure a return to bondage.

Biblical Separation

God has never called His people to be like the world in any area of their lives. He has never called them to blend in. The nation of Israel is a type and shadow of the church, and throughout its history God required them to be different from the world. Many books in the Bible teach God's people to separate themselves from the world. From cover to cover, God in His Word calls His people to be different from the world, to rise above the status quo and stand for Him!

- *"Now the Lord had said unto Abram, Get thee out of thy country, and from thy kindred" (Genesis 12:1).*

- *"And ye shall be holy unto me: for I the Lord am*

holy, and have severed you from other people, that ye should be mine" (Leviticus 20:26).

- *"Thou shalt make no covenant with them. . . . For thou art an holy people unto the LORD thy God: the LORD thy God hath chosen thee to be a special people unto himself, above all people that are upon the face of the earth" (Deuteronomy 7:2, 6).*

- *"For thou art an holy people unto the LORD thy God, and the LORD hath chosen thee to be a peculiar people unto himself, above all the nations that are upon the earth" (Deuteronomy 14:2).*

- *"That ye come not among these nations, these that remain among you; neither make mention of the name of their gods, nor cause to swear by them, neither serve them, nor bow yourselves unto them: but cleave unto the LORD your God, as ye have done unto this day" (Joshua 23:7-8).*

- *"And ye shall make no league with the inhabitants of this land; ye shall throw down their altars" (Judges 2:2).*

- *"Now therefore make confession unto the LORD God of your fathers, and do his pleasure: and separate yourselves from the people of the land, and from the strange wives" (Ezra 10:11).*

- *"When they had heard the law . . . they separated from Israel all the mixed multitude" (Nehemiah 13:3).*

- *"Blessed is the man that walketh not in the counsel of the ungodly, nor standeth in the way of sinners, nor sitteth in the seat of the scornful" (Psalm 1:1).*

- *"Depart ye, depart ye, go ye out from thence, touch no unclean thing; go ye out of the midst of her; be ye clean, that bear the vessels of the LORD" (Isaiah 52:11).*

Sometimes it is said that the call for separation is only in the Old Testament, but that is not true. Jesus Christ wanted His New Testament church to be separate from the world.

- *"Because ye are not of the world, but I have chosen you out of the world, therefore the world hateth you" (John 15:19).*

- *"Save yourselves from this untoward generation" (Acts 2:40).*

- *"Be not conformed to this world, but be ye transformed" (Romans 12:2).*

- *"What fellowship hath righteousness with unrighteousness? and what communion hath light with darkness? . . . Wherefore come out from among them, and be ye separate, saith the Lord, and touch not the unclean thing; and I will receive you" (II Corinthians 6:14, 17).*

- *"And have no fellowship with the unfruitful works of darkness, but rather reprove them" (Ephesians 5:11).*

- *"Know ye not that the friendship of the world is enmity with God?"* (James 4:4).

- *"But ye are a chosen generation, a royal priesthood, an holy nation, a peculiar people; that ye should shew forth the praises of him who hath called you out of darkness into his marvellous light"* (I Peter 2:9).

There is too much in Scripture on the subject of separation to ignore it. The church is clearly commanded to live separate from the world. If we look like the world and do everything the world does, can we possibly be separated?

Love Not the World

I John is a small yet powerful book in the New Testament that clearly states the doctrine of Christian love:

"Herein is love, not that we loved God, but that he loved us. . . . Beloved, if God so loved us, we ought also to love one another. . . . We love him, because he first loved us. If a man say, I love God, and hateth his brother, he is a liar" (I John 4:10, 11, 19-20).

The three themes of love are:
    1. God's love for humanity

2. Our love for God
3. Brother's love for brother

Without question, the Christian is to love God and his neighbor, but the writer clearly prefaced all his remarks with a call to **reject cultural society**:

"Love not the world, neither the things that are in the world. If any man love the world, the love of the Father is not in him. For all that is in the world, the lust of the flesh, and the lust of the eyes, and the pride of life, is not of the Father, but is of the world" (I John 2:15-16).

A clear line is drawn between loving one another and loving the world. The world outside the church is dominated by the lust of the flesh, the lust of the eye, and the pride of life, and Christians are strongly instructed to keep themselves from it. John was aware of the attractiveness and lure of the world and admonished the church in no uncertain terms to have no love for the things of the world. There should be no common ground between the world and the church.

Never should we interpret any of the separation passages to mean a hatred for people, for we are instructed to love the sinner. Loving the world in the sense of caring for each individual person is essential, but we must never love the things of the world, the kingdoms controlled by Satan.

Conclusion

As a child, I dreamed of how thrilling it would have been to stand with David and face Goliath while the armies ran, or Daniel at the prayer window while the lions roared, or perhaps Rahab as she stood at the window with a scarlet thread while Jericho laughed at her faith, or the Christians in the Roman Coliseum refusing to denounce their beliefs. They were real heroes who faced enormous obstacles yet remained faithful.

I have lived to see the day when I have the opportunity to do what they did in a small measure. Along with the three young men on the plain of Dura, I have the option to stand or bow. Now that my faith costs me something, am I willing to pay the price? Yes, a thousand times, yes, by the grace of God!

Winston Churchill and his advisers met in closed sessions during World War II to assess their situation and map out their strategies. Adviser after adviser stood and told of shortages, weaknesses, outages, example after example of all that was inadequate with their resources. Winston Churchill looked into their bleak and discouraged faces and declared, "Gentlemen, I find it all rather inspiring."

For those of us still standing, our task is enormous and our resources are limited. Strong armies in the spirit world march against us, and our words are often drowned out by the loud clamor of others. Regardless, I have decided to stand. In fact, I find it all rather inspiring.

In 1989, our daughter Alyson, a member of the concert band of our high school, was asked to march in the Barberton Cherry Blossom Parade with the Barberton High School band. She was a freshman in high school, and it was an honor to be included. She happily consented, but there was a problem. The band uniforms were all slacks, and Alyson wore only skirts and dresses. Maintaining a difference between male and female in dress is very important to our family and our church.

Though the Band Boosters, the band's financial backers, were opposed, the director made his decision. The Apostolic girl could wear a matching, modest-length majorette skirt and march in the band. It had never been done before in the history of Barberton High School.

Alyson has graduated from college now, and I am certain she will accomplish great things with her life, but the day she marched down the streets of Barberton in that skirt playing her glockenspiel, while the rest of the band wore slacks, was one of her finest hours. She did not march in arrogance, spiritual pride or contempt, but she marched with convictions, and the world took notice.

And as for me, it *was* my finest hour, for I saw in Alyson the future for all of us who have remained standing amidst the world's commands to bow. There will always be those who bow, but there will always be those who refuse to bow. Alyson marched, smiling, strong of faith and standing for righteousness. I wept because of her bravery.

Johann Goethe wrote in *Conversations with Eckerman*, "Give us your convictions! As for doubts, we have enough of our own already." While the world's systems and institutions are pushing us to conform to the pressures of the world, there are people in the world who long to see men and women with convictions who will refuse the world's pushing and bullying and will stand uncompromisingly. They long for someone to have unyielding faith in Christian principles, for they hear doubts continually from every side. Hungry humanity has never given its ear to a church marching to the same drummer as they do. They look for the man or woman who hears the beat of a different drummer.

> While the world's systems and institutions are pushing us to conform to the pressures of the world, there are people in the world who long to see men and women with convictions.

I intend to keep marching with every single conviction intact. Everyone will not understand. I may be told I look ugly and out of style, but I am not bowing down. I may be accused of being a legalist and being pharisaical, but I am not bowing down. I may be told these issues are insignificant and irrelevant to the masses, but I am not bowing down. I may be scoffed at, misunderstood, and accused of being all sorts of things, but my final declaration must be the same as the three Hebrew children, Mordecai and the Lord Jesus Christ: "I will not bow."

Alyson, in her modest-length skirt, marching in the band.